THIS LIFE WITH ANIMALS BOOK BELONGS TO:

_____

Saving Schmiddy

A Life With Animals Adventure

by
Andi Lehman

Illustrations by Marlon at GetYourBookIllustrations

"Those who wish to pet and baby wild animals 'love' them.
But those who respect their natures and wish to let them live normal lives love them more."
Edwin Way Teale

Copyright © 2022 Andi Lehman
All Rights Reserved
Publisher: Wilderland Press

Printed in the United States of America
Book Design by Kezia
Illustrations by Marlon
www.getyourbookillustrations.com

Publisher's Cataloging-in-Publication data

Names: Lehman, Andi, author.
Title: Saving Schmiddy : a life with animals adventure / by Andi Lehman.
Description: Hernando, MS: Wilderland Press, 2022. | Summary: A caring boy rescues an injured speckled kingsnake and helps his fearful mom appreciate and value all snakes as he learns more about them.
Identifiers: LCCN: 2022919391 | ISBN: 979-8-9870961-1-6 (hardcover) | 979-8-9870961-0-9 (paperback) | 979-8-9870961-2-3 (ebook)
Subjects: LCSH Snakes--Juvenile literature. | Lampropeltis--Juvenile literature. | Wildlife rehabilitation--Juvenile literature. | CYAC Snakes. | Kingsnakes. | Wildlife rehabilitation. | BISAC JUVENILE NONFICTION / Animals / Reptiles & Amphibians
Classification: LCC QL666.O636 .L44 2022 | DDC 597.96--dc23

In loving memory of my mother, Joanne Yates Boucher,
who taught me to care about all God's creatures,
and Joy, who lived up to her name.

Thanks to my best encourager, Marylane Wade Koch; my brilliant and generous mentors, Dr. Shannon McGee and Terry Vandeventer; the amazing creative team at GYBI, Karen Ferreira, Marlon, Kezia, Jitendra, and Po; dedicated animal advocates and rehabilitators everywhere, including Nancy Fachman, Petra May, James Bryant, Dr. Lynn Cox, Lindsi and Korey Wilson, Tammy Nash, Ginger Vandeventer, and Chris Baker; kind advisors, Darcy Pattison, Gaye Clark, and Elizabeth Law; my friends at the First Regional libraries, Collierville Animal Clinic, KCWCG, Petco, and Repticon; and especially to Dan, Reyn, and Russ, who share and support my life with animals.

Although Schmiddy was handled often, and even massaged as part of her physical therapy, most wild animals are handled as little as possible during rehabilitation.

Schmiddy

Bitsy

Although Bitsy observes Schmiddy's journey throughout the book, pets are always kept away from wildlife during rehabilitation.

Speckled Kingsnake Classification

Kingdom: Animalia

Phylum: Chordata

Class: Reptilia

Order: Squamata

Suborder: Serpentes

Family: Colubridae

Genus: Lampropeltis

Species/Scientific name: Lampropeltis holbrooki

Common name: Speckled kingsnake

Nickname: Salt and Pepper snake

Website

"In the end, we will conserve only what we love,

We will love only what we understand,

And we will understand only what we are taught."

Babo Dioum

On a cold fall day in Hernando, Mississippi, Dad and I find a snake. Well, half a snake. We lift some logs to see the rest of him.
"He's nearly frozen," Dad says. "Let's go inside and warm him up."

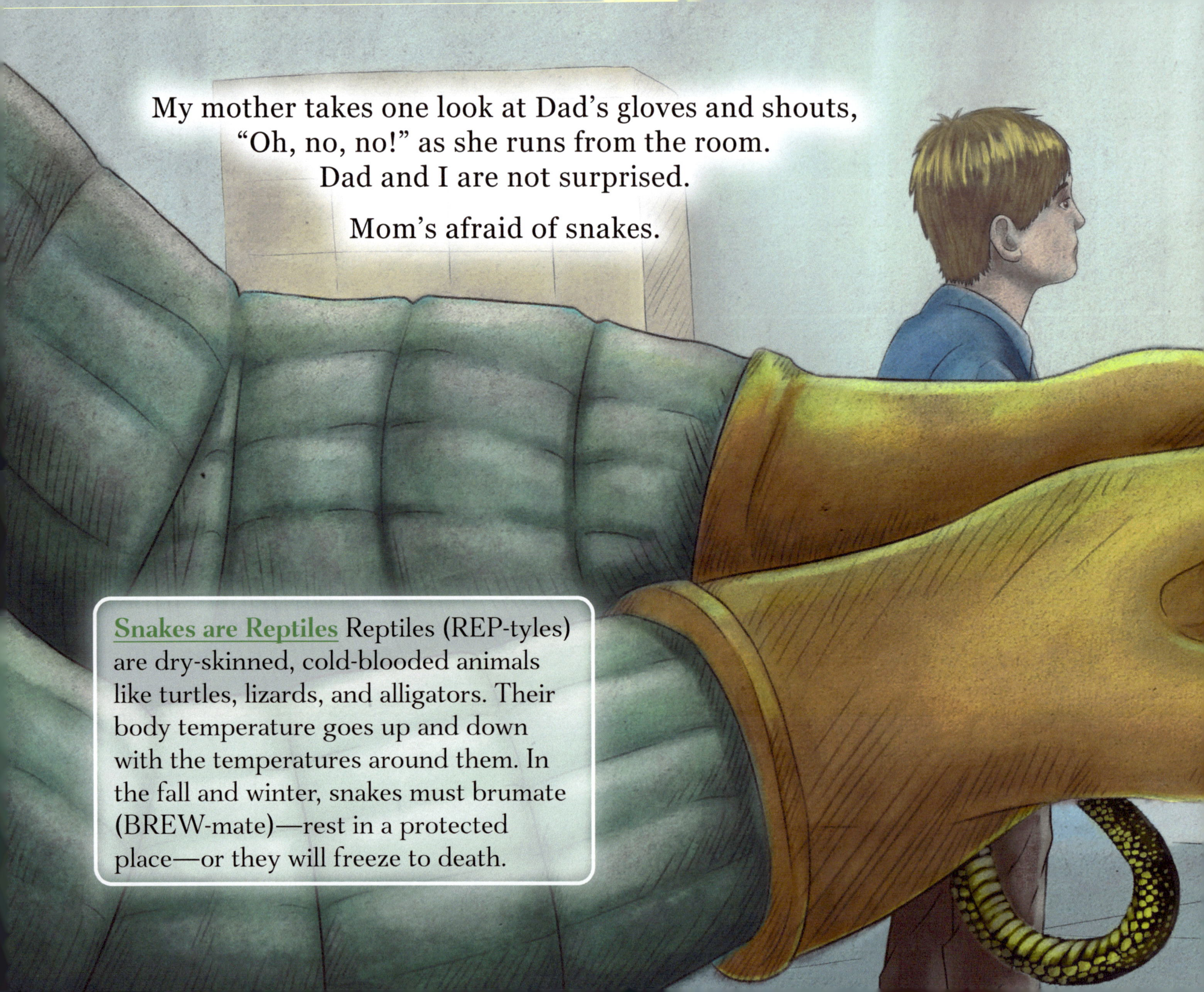

My mother takes one look at Dad's gloves and shouts, "Oh, no, no!" as she runs from the room.
Dad and I are not surprised.

Mom's afraid of snakes.

Snakes are Reptiles Reptiles (REP-tyles) are dry-skinned, cold-blooded animals like turtles, lizards, and alligators. Their body temperature goes up and down with the temperatures around them. In the fall and winter, snakes must brumate (BREW-mate)—rest in a protected place—or they will freeze to death.

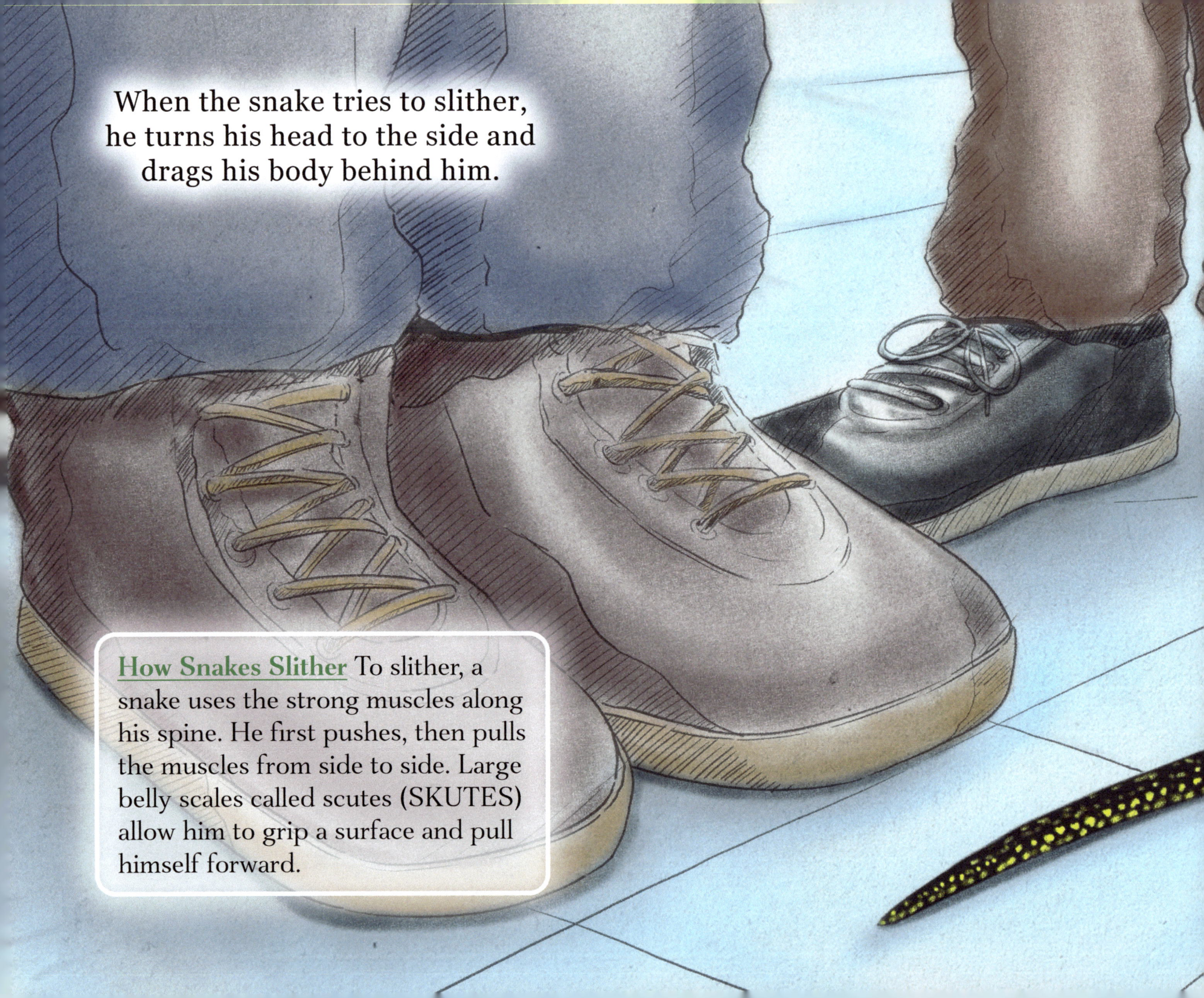

When the snake tries to slither, he turns his head to the side and drags his body behind him.

How Snakes Slither To slither, a snake uses the strong muscles along his spine. He first pushes, then pulls the muscles from side to side. Large belly scales called scutes (SKUTES) allow him to grip a surface and pull himself forward.

"Mom will know what to do," I say. She rescues animals and teaches people how to help them.

Will she help a sick snake?

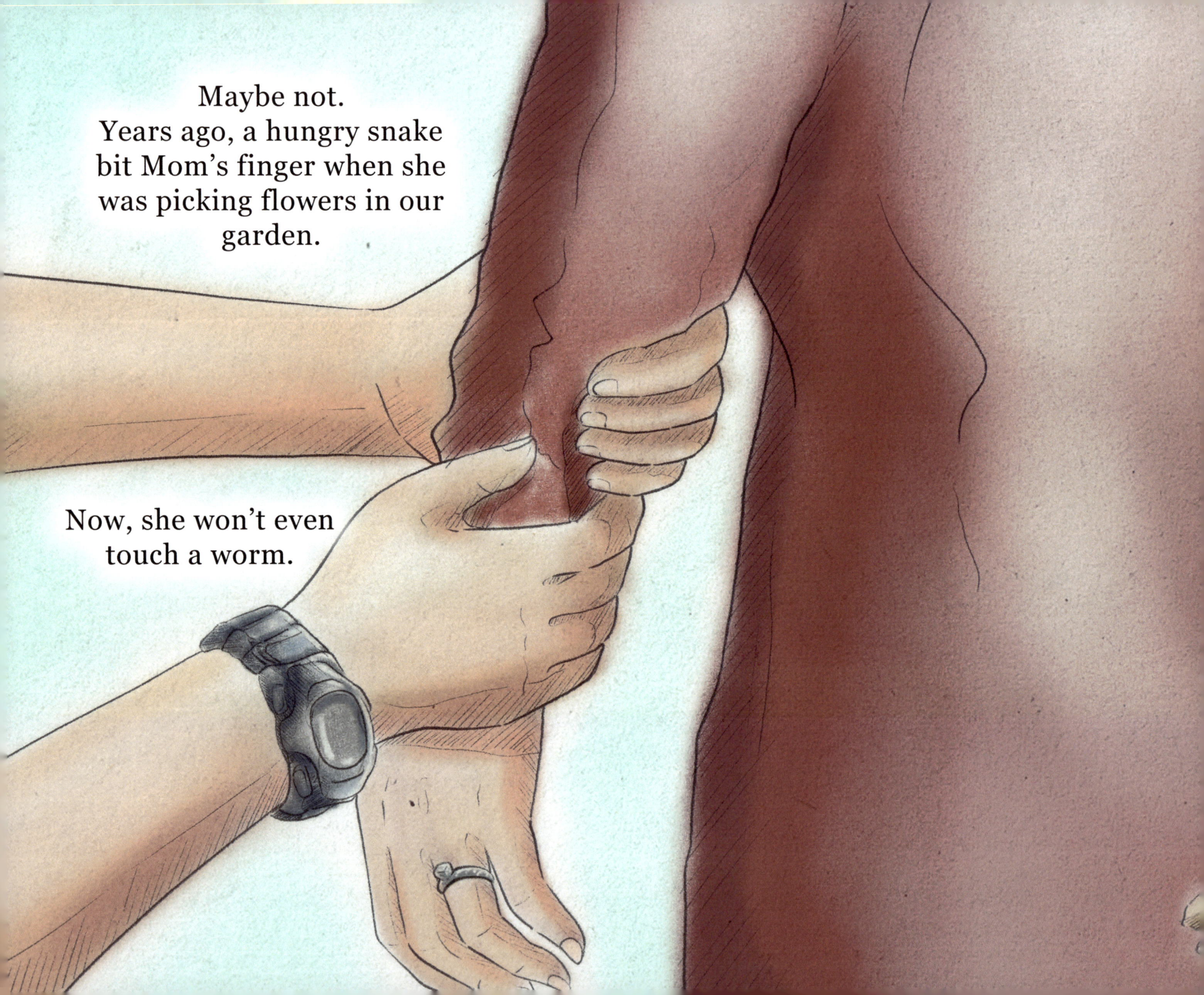

"Mom, the snake is hurt," I say.
"Please come see him."
She shakes her head. "I can't!"
"Yes, you can," I say, and I pull her toward the kitchen.

Snake Bites Snakes only bite to grip their prey (PRAY)—the animals they hunt—or to defend themselves. Most people who get bitten by snakes are trying to kill or bother them. In the US, only four to six people die each year from a snake bite, but fifty to sixty people die annually from flying insect stings.

Her hand sweats in mine as she peeks at the snake. "I think his back is broken," she says. "He needs an X-ray."

How Snakes Eat Snakes are carnivores (CAR-nih-vohrs) or meat-eaters. Their jaws can stretch to eat an animal three or four times wider than their body width. All snakes have teeth to help hold their food or kill it. Some snakes called constrictors (cuhn-STRICK-ters) coil around their prey and suffocate it by squeezing.

The snake lies quiet as we drive. I wonder if he knows I'm trying to save him.

A Snake's Life The life span of a snake depends on the species (SPEE-sheez/SPEE-seez) or the kind of snake. Large snakes usually live longer than small ones. Except when they mate, most snakes are shy and travel alone. They don't interact with people unless they are startled or threatened.

The veterinarian says our patient is a "salt and pepper" snake—a harmless speckled king. On the X-ray, we see the crack in the snake's spine.

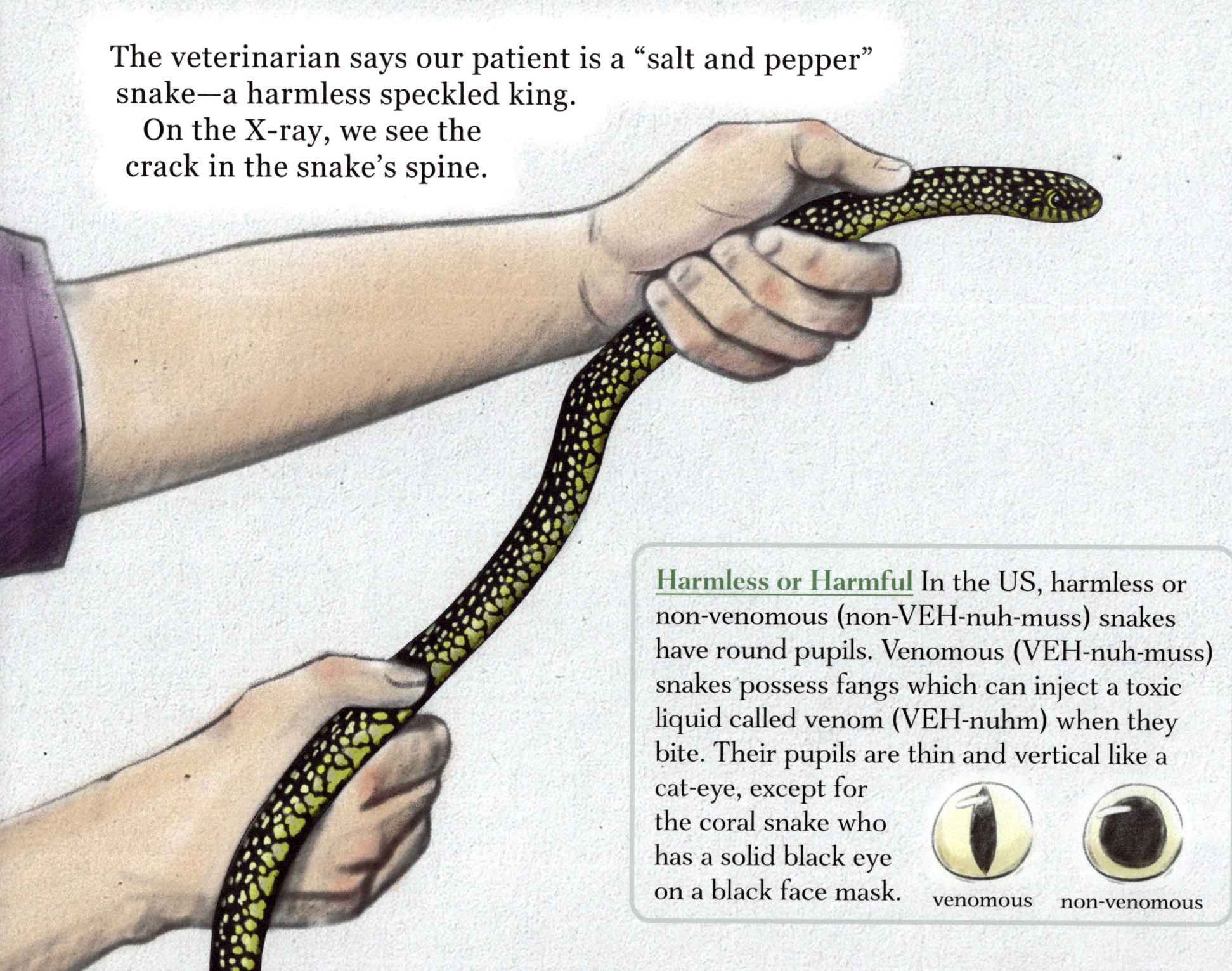

Harmless or Harmful In the US, harmless or non-venomous (non-VEH-nuh-muss) snakes have round pupils. Venomous (VEH-nuh-muss) snakes possess fangs which can inject a toxic liquid called venom (VEH-nuhm) when they bite. Their pupils are thin and vertical like a cat-eye, except for the coral snake who has a solid black eye on a black face mask.

venomous   non-venomous

I smile at Mom.

I'm not afraid of snakes.

Inside a Snake Snakes have most of the same organs people do but only one working lung. In tube feeding, a thin tube goes down the esophagus (ee-SOF-uh-guss)—a canal connecting the throat to the snake's gut—so liquid food or medicine can be put directly into his stomach.

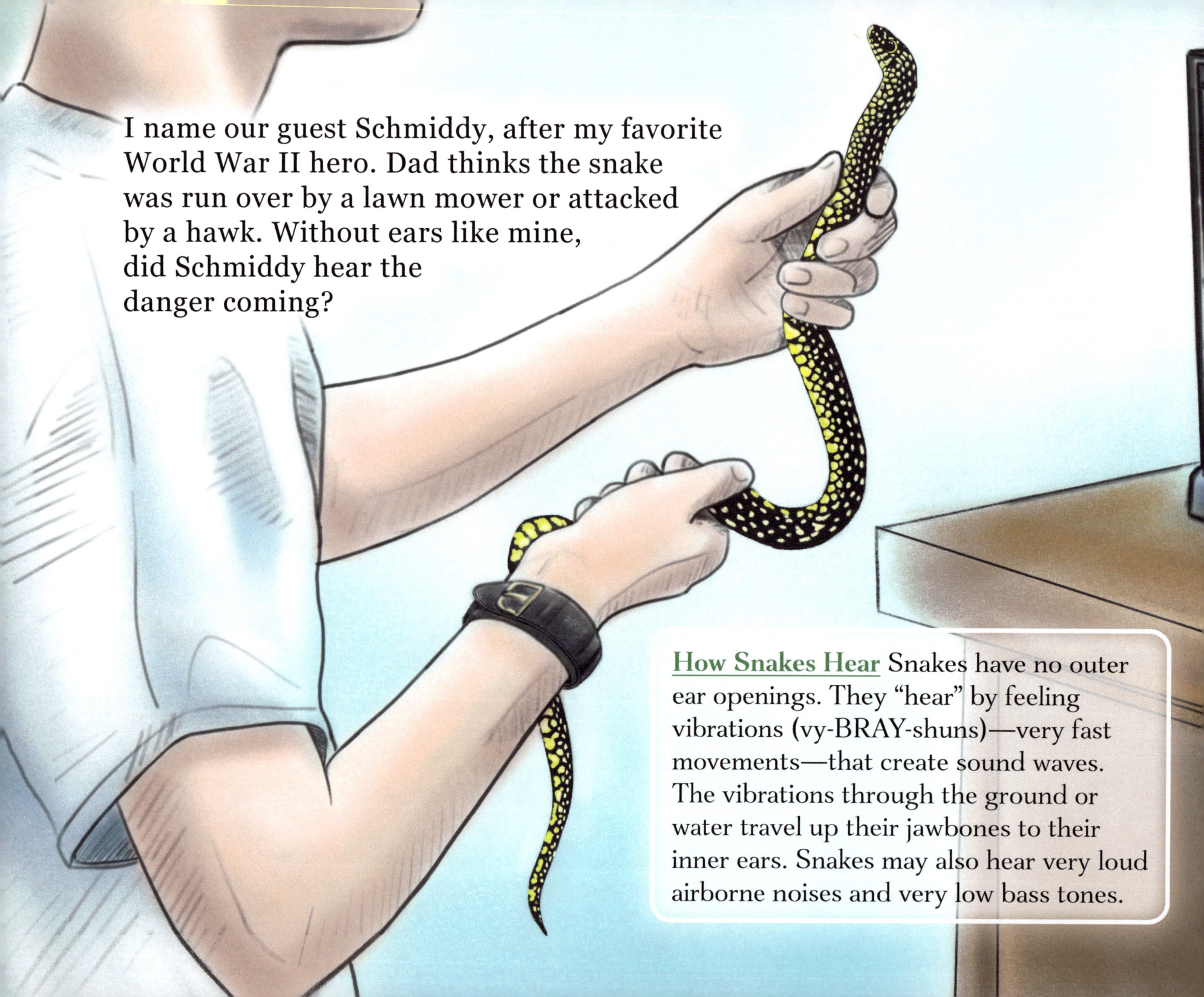

I name our guest Schmiddy, after my favorite World War II hero. Dad thinks the snake was run over by a lawn mower or attacked by a hawk. Without ears like mine, did Schmiddy hear the danger coming?

How Snakes Hear Snakes have no outer ear openings. They "hear" by feeling vibrations (vy-BRAY-shuns)—very fast movements—that create sound waves. The vibrations through the ground or water travel up their jawbones to their inner ears. Snakes may also hear very loud airborne noises and very low bass tones.

While I set up his new home, Mom gives me a warning from the hall. "If that snake escapes, I'm closing your bedroom door—forever!"

Each morning, I give Schmiddy fresh water. He never tries to bite me. I check the sticky heat pad under one side of his tank to make sure it's working so he can choose to be warm or cold.

Snake Defenses Besides biting, snakes have four defenses—fleeing, hiding, shaking their tails, or releasing a stinky substance called musk. A snake expels the musk, as well as waste, through an opening called the vent on his underbelly where the tail begins.

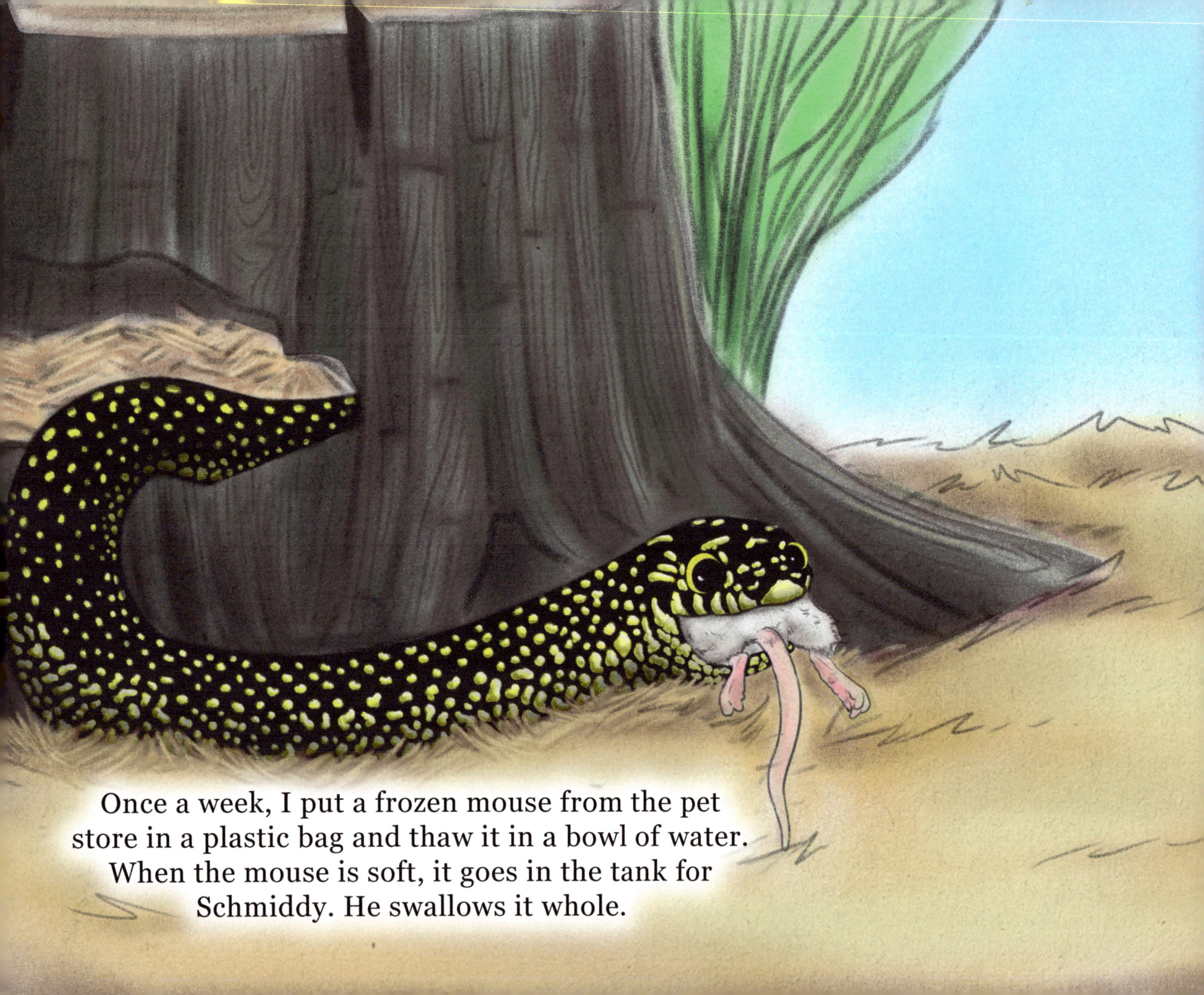

Once a week, I put a frozen mouse from the pet store in a plastic bag and thaw it in a bowl of water. When the mouse is soft, it goes in the tank for Schmiddy. He swallows it whole.

He likes to slip like a rope through my fingers or curl up in my clothes. His red tongue flicks in and out. Mom tells me I'm a good rehabber—a caregiver for animals.

I hope Schmiddy agrees.

A Tongue for Exploring Snakes breathe air through their noses, but they smell with their tongues. The snake's forked tongue picks up scents from the air and brings them back to a special organ on the roof of his mouth. This Jacobson's (JAY-cub-suns) organ helps the snake identify whatever he smells.

At the library, we learn how snakes protect our food supply by hunting the rats and mice that munch on our crops.

Scarlet kingsnake

Speckled kingsnake

How Snakes Hunt Snakes kill more rodents (ROH-dents)— small mammals like mice and rats— than all the other rodent-eating animals combined. Most snakes see well to hunt. Some snakes called pit vipers also "see" using special holes or pits along their jawline that can sense heat. The heat pits help the snakes find warm-blooded prey.

Mom says we can thank a farmer— and a snake—for pizza, brownies, and birthday cake.

After a few weeks, my mother surprises me.
She wants to touch Schmiddy.
She puts two fingers behind his head and slides them toward his tail.
"He's not slimy," she says. "He's smooth and cool!"

I show her how to hold him with both hands and support his spine.
"I'm proud of you," I say.
She grins.

Skin Deep Beauty
A snake's skin can be smooth or keeled (KEE-uhld)—rough and bumpy. Snakes come in as many colors and patterns as butterflies and birds. They may be one solid color or have markings like stripes, speckles, or bands.

Two months later, Schmiddy's skin fades, and his eyes grow cloudy. He needs to shed his skin, but when he tries, he only rubs away a few small pieces.

Eyes of "Blue" A snake's eyes are protected by permanent see-through scales called spectacles or brilles (BRILLS.) Before shedding, his eyes turn milky blue, and he can't see well—a condition called blueing. His body is also sensitive to touch. About four times a year, adult snakes must shed their skin to grow and to replace dead cells.

Success!

After the soak, I slide the old skin down Schmiddy's back like I peel off my socks—inside out.
I wave his shed around like a flag to celebrate. Mom laughs.

The partial skin hangs on my bulletin board until my sister's dog spies it one afternoon
and eats it.

Shedding Skin, Not Scales
Snakes are covered in scales (SCAY-uhls)—tiny bumps attached to their skin that protect their bodies and organs. Three skin layers cover the scales: a colored bottom layer and a middle and top layer that are clear. When the top layer peels away, the middle layer takes its place, and the shed is complete.

Although Schmiddy gets better, he can't return to the woods. He may always need help to shed, and he doesn't move fast enough to catch his own dinner.

Who Scares Whom? Natural enemies or predators (PREH-duh-turs) of snakes include dogs, cats, raptors, coyotes, foxes, racoons, alligators, skunks, bobcats, and other snakes. Snakes also get crushed beneath cars or bulldozers or killed by frightened homeowners. Snakes have good reasons to fear people, and they do.

By the end of our visit, most people change their minds.

The Three Rs of Wildlife Rescue In the US, licensed rescue groups and their volunteers raise orphaned baby animals, rehabilitate (ree-huh-BIL-ih-tate) or help to heal injured animals, and release them back into the wild. States pass laws to protect mammals and reptiles. Native birds are protected by federal laws.

Just like Mom.

In June, a reptile expert from the Natural Museum of Science examines our education snake at an outdoor festival in Jackson. He shares some interesting news—Schmiddy is a girl.

The real Schmiddy was Marine Corps Private Albert (Al) Schmid. He and his friend, Corporal Leroy Diamond, earned the Navy Cross for their bravery in battle on Guadalcanal (GWAH-duhl-cuh-NAAL.) Leroy's injuries healed, but Al Schmid was blind for the rest of his life.

It's a Girl! Without a special examination, it's hard to tell if a snake is male or female. In some species, females have short, thick tails while males have longer, thin ones. Most female snakes lay eggs, but some, like copperheads, rattlesnakes, and cottonmouths, give birth to live young.

Now retired, Schmiddy lives a quiet life on our small farm in Mississippi.
My mother continues to help animals and teach people to care about them. She works with lots of different species, including fifteen reptiles.

I'm still not afraid of snakes.

And neither is Mom.

Mom with milk snake, Hollywood

Russ with corn snake, Aracorn

Exclusive Content
Meet Schmiddy!

Author's Note

I chose to write this true story through the voice of my son, James Russell, who lived the adventure of saving Schmiddy. I am grateful to him and Schmiddy for teaching me not only to value snakes but also to love them.

Andi Lehman

More About Snakes

- All snakes have spines with as many as 200 small bones called vertebrae (VER-tuh-bray.)
- All snakes can swim.
- Snakes don't have eyelids, so they can't blink. They sleep with their eyes open.
- Some snakes can "fly" or glide by throwing themselves into the air and twisting.
- Snakes that regularly climb trees or live in them are called arboreal (ar-BOHR-ee-uhl.)
- Desert snakes move through sand by leaping sideways or sidewinding (SIDE-wyn-ding.)
- Most snakes are diurnal (dy-ER-nuhl) or active during the day and prefer temperatures between 75-80 degrees Fahrenheit.
- Snake eggs are laid in a group called a clutch. They are oval shaped and rubbery.

SNAKES AROUND THE WORLD

So far, scientists have identified over 3000 kinds of snakes on earth, including 600 venomous species of which only 200 are dangerous or deadly to human beings. Snakes live everywhere except Antarctica, Ireland, Greenland, New Zealand, and Iceland.

The smallest snake we know of is the four-inch thread snake also called a blind or worm snake. The longest snake is the reticulated (ruh-TIC-you-lay-ted) python at thirty-two feet. The heaviest snake is the 600-pound anaconda (an-uh-CON-duh.)

Boas, pythons, and colubrids (cuh-LEW-brids) are all constrictors. Most snakes are loners, but red-sided garter snakes share a den in winter.

SNAKES IN THE UNITED STATES

More than 130 known snake species live in the USA, of which less than thirty are venomous.

Several snakes in the US are endangered (ehn-DANE-jerd), or close to disappearing forever, like the beautiful San Francisco garter snake and the indigo snake, our largest native species, which grows up to nine feet.

Benjamin Franklin wanted a Timber rattlesnake—or a turkey—to be the US animal symbol.

SPECKLED KINGSNAKES: MADE IN AMERICA

Speckled kings are endemic (ehn-DEM-ick) to, or only found in, the mid and south-eastern US. They range from Iowa and Nebraska down through Kansas and Oklahoma to west-central Texas and across to the east through Missouri, Arkansas, Louisiana, Mississippi, and Alabama. They prefer habitats around bodies of water like rivers or swamps.

Kingsnakes belong to the group of constrictors called colubrids (cuh-LEW-brids) which includes over 1000 species. The snake's name, Lampropeltis holbrooki, comes from his smooth, glossy scales and an American herpetologist. "Lampris" is the Greek word for shiny, and "pelte" means shield. In 1942, John Edwards Holbrook was the first to describe and document a speckled king.

The conservation status of speckled kings is "least concern" with 100,000 or more in the US, but in some states it's illegal to sell, buy, or capture speckled kings, and in Iowa, they are considered a threatened species. In the wild, they can live to be over twenty years old.

Speckled kings breed in April or May. Females can lay between six and twenty-three eggs. All kingsnakes help balance the populations of rodents, frogs, and other snakes.

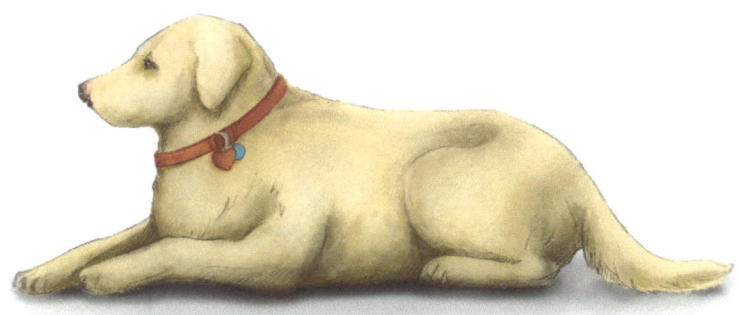

VENOMOUS SNAKES

Venomous snakes can have front or rear fangs—two enlarged teeth that inject venom.

Some cobras can also spit venom from their fangs.

Snake venom is used in several medicines to fight pain or illnesses like cancer and heart disease as well as to treat venomous snake bites.

Venomous snakes in the US include the coral snake and the pit vipers—rattlesnakes, copperheads, and cottonmouths (also called water moccasins.)

Pit vipers have cat-eye or elliptical (ee-LIP-tick-uhl) pupils.

Several snakes in the US have red, black, and yellow bands. On the skin pattern of the venomous coral snake, red and yellow bands touch—"Red and yellow will kill a fellow."

On the skin pattern of non-venomous mimics like the harmless scarlet king or milk snake, red and black bands touch—"Red and black is a friend to Jack."

The only US venomous water snake is the yellow-bellied sea snake, found in Pacific waters off the west coast or near the Hawaiian Islands. Like pit vipers, this species bears live young.

Black Mambas are the deadliest venomous snakes in the world.

WILD SNAKES AND PET SNAKES

If you see a wild snake, take two steps backwards and walk away. Be kind. Give a snake a break!

Wild snakes belong in the wild. Pet stores or reptile expos sell captive-bred snakes for pets.

Purchased snakes need water, proper food, a clean habitat, and regular handling to be good pets.

SNAKE SMILES

Why are snakes so hard to fool?
Because you can't pull their legs.

How do snakes know how much they weigh?
They have their own scales.

Why was the snake at the computer?
He was looking for the mouse.

COMING SOON
Another Life With Animals tale, Rescuing Roufus

ABOUT THE AUTHOR

Andi Lehman has over thirty years of experience as a dedicated animal advocate, rehabilitator, and rescuer in Mississippi, Tennessee, and Pennsylvania. An eclectic writer and enthusiastic conservationist, she penned the land lease grant proposal that launched the ARK: Arkabutla Lake Wildlife Rehabilitation and Nature Center in Hernando, MS.

Through her company, Life with Animals, Andi promotes the wonder and value of all creatures—domestic, native, or exotic—and our responsibility to them. She lives in Mississippi with her family and twenty-seven critters, most of whom appear in the popular education programs she has created. To learn more about Andi's continuing work with words and wildlife, visit AndiLehman.com.

ABOUT THE ILLUSTRATOR

GetYourBookIllustrations was founded in South Africa in 2016 with the purpose of assisting authors to illustrate and publish beautiful and professional books. It all started with Karen Ferreira's passion for helping other writers around the world enjoy amazing and affordable artwork in their children's literature.

GetYourBookIllustrations now employs over fifteen professional illustrators, including Marlon, the talented artist who worked on Saving Schmiddy. For more information, visit GetYourBookIllustrations.com.

www.ingramcontent.com/pod-product-compliance
Lightning Source LLC
Chambersburg PA
CBHW041554030426
42337CB00004B/51